PIONEERS OF ENGLISH FOLK GUITAR

WISE PUBLICATIONS
part of The Music Sales Group
London / New York / Paris / Sydney / Copenhagen / Berlin / Madrid /Hong Kong/ Tokyo

Published by
Wise Publications
14-15 Berners Street,
London W1T 3LJ, UK.

Exclusive Distributors:
Music Sales Limited
Distribution Centre, Newmarket Road,
Bury St Edmunds, Suffolk IP33 3YB, UK.
Music Sales Corporation
257 Park Avenue South,
New York, NY 10010, USA.
Music Sales Pty Limited
20 Resolution Drive, Caringbah,
NSW 2229, Australia.

Order No. AM1003805
ISBN 978-1-78038-199-2

Edited by Adrian Hopkins.
Cover design by Ruth Keating.

Photos courtesy of:
Artist: Bert Jansch (Estate Of Keith Morris/Redferns/Getty Images)
Davey Graham (Photo by Brian Shuel/Redferns)
Gordon Giltrap (Photo by Gems/Redferns)
Jake Thackray (Photo by David Magnus/Rex Features)
John Martyn (Photo by Brian Cooke/Redferns)
John Renbourn (Photo by Dave Peabody/Redferns)
Martin Carthy (Photo by Brian Shuel/Redferns)
Nic Jones (Photo by Dave Peabody/Redferns)
Nick Drake (Photo by GAB Archive/Redferns)
Richard Thompson (Photo by David Redfern/Redferns)

Printed in the EU.

Your Guarantee of Quality
As publishers, we strive to produce every book to the
highest commercial standards.
This book has been carefully designed to minimise awkward
page turns and to make playing from it a real pleasure.
Particular care has been given to specifying acid-free, neutral-sized paper
made from pulps which have not been elemental chlorine bleached.
This pulp is from farmed sustainable forests and was
produced with special regard for the environment.
Throughout, the printing and binding have been planned to
ensure a sturdy, attractive publication which should give years of enjoyment.
If your copy fails to meet our high standards,
please inform us and we will gladly replace it.

www.musicsales.com

1952 VINCENT BLACK LIGHTNING

RICHARD THOMPSON

Original release: *Rumor and Sigh* (1991)

Born in Notting Hill in 1949, Richard Thompson has long been a highly-regarded guitarist and songwriter. After being spotted in 1967 playing with Fairport Convention he was signed to Island Records and went on to record five albums with the band including the classic *Liege And Lief*. After session work with artists including Nick Drake, he embarked on a solo career, which to date has produced over 30 albums. '1952 Vincent Black Lightning' (the most requested song on PBS radio in America) is played in one of Thompson's favourite tunings (CGDGBE) with a thumb pick. Concentrate on maintaining a steady bass line rhythm throughout.

ANJI

DAVEY GRAHAM

Original release: *3/4 AD* (1962)

Practically a rite of passage for any self-respecting guitarist, 'Anji' has been covered by Gordon Giltrap, John Renbourn, Bert Jansch, Paul Simon and many others. During the early 1960s, only John Fahey was playing guitar instrumentals to any acclaim. 'Anji' was to spread throughout the folk community, changing its name as it went ('Angi', 'Angie', etc.). 'Streets Of London' songwriter Ralph Mctell said: "The hard part of this was that there were two beats to every bass note instead of the one that most of us were able to play."

BLACK WATERSIDE

GORDON GILTRAP

Original release: _Janschology_ (2000)

Like several other pieces in this compilation, 'Black Waterside' has been adapted by many musicians. An early rendition was by Mary Doran in 1952, which then passed through several players' repertoires until it appeared on Bert Jansch's _Jack Orion_ in 1965. Giltrap's version showcases his fine abilities as a soloist, especially throughout the semiquaver triplets in the coda.

CANADEE-I-O

NIC JONES

Original release: _Penguin Eggs_ (1979)

In 2001 _Penguin Eggs_ was awarded 2nd place (behind _Liege And Lief_) in the 'Best folk album of all time' category by listeners of the Mike Harding show on BBC Radio 2. 'Canadee-i-o' was also recorded by Bob Dylan on his 1992 album _Good As I Been To You_. An important feature of Jones' intricate style — he acknowledges Martin Carthy as a key influence — is a regular percussive sound made by striking downwards with the middle and ring fingers of the right hand on damped bass strings close to or above the bridge of the guitar. This is similar to the 'frailing' technique used by banjo players.

THE HERMIT

JOHN RENBOURN

Original release: _The Hermit_ (1976)

Although commonly labelled a folk guitarist, John Renbourn's influences include early music, classical, blues and world music. He first met Bert Jansch in the early 1960s, and has recorded with him both as a duo and as part of Pentangle. Considered one of Renbourn's finest albums, _The Hermit_ displays his compositional talents throughout. Look out for the harmonics on the ninth fret, as they may take a little practice to achieve the best tone.

MAY YOU NEVER

JOHN MARTYN

Original release: _Solid Air_ (1973)

Taken from Martyn's most enduring album, 'May You Never' (like 'Anji') is truly a standard of the modern folk guitar. Always a favourite at Martyn's concerts, this has been recorded by many artists including Sandi Thom and Eric Clapton. An early example of 'folk-fusion', many styles are successfully merged throughout this song. Martyn played with a mixture of fingerstyle and percussive slap to give additional rhythm to the accompaniment.

MY BABY SO SWEET

NICK DRAKE

Original release: _Family Tree_ (2007)

Although bootlegged for many years from Drake's own home demos, this song was not to receive an official release until 2007. Drake's albums sold poorly in his lifetime, but he is now considered one of the most influential singer-songwriters of the past 50 years. A self-taught guitarist, he achieved his style through the use of alternative tunings to create cluster chords, which are difficult to achieve on a guitar in standard tuning.

ON AGAIN! ON AGAIN!

JAKE THACKRAY

Original release: _On Again! On Again!_ (1977)

This bawdy tale of a long-suffering husband shows off Thackray's lugubrious voice, and his flair for a witty lyric. His strong Yorkshire accent and the northern setting of many of his songs led to him being described as the North country Noël Coward, although he insisted that his strongest influences came from the French chansoniers, in particular Georges Brassens.

Strolling Down The Highway

BERT JANSCH

Original release: _Bert Jansch_ (1965)

Also covered by Nick Drake on _Family Tree_, this was the first song on Jansch's self-titled debut album. His musical influences are wide-ranging: American bluesmen such as Big Bill Broonzy and Brownie McGhee, folk singers Anne Briggs and A. L. Lloyd, and jazz musicians such as Charles Mingus and Jimmy Giuffre all strongly influenced Jansch's early output. He has gone on to release over 30 albums and influence many different guitarists, including Jimmy Page, Bernard Butler and Johnny Marr.

The Whale Catchers

MARTIN CARTHY

Original release: _A Selection from The Penguin Book of English Folk Songs_ (1986)

Martin Carthy has been one of the most influential figures in British traditional music ever since his emergence during the folk revival of the early '60s. His style is marked by a strong percussive feel, emphasising the melody, and his use of unusual tunings. In 'The Whale Catchers', his guitar is tuned to CGCDGA. This encourages 'vertical' playing: melodies are mostly found by moving up and down the length of the string, instead of crossing from one string to another. This vertical technique is usually accomplished by two strings in tandem with occasional 'help' from neighbouring strings.

GUITAR TABLATURE EXPLAINED

Guitar music can be notated in three different ways: on a musical stave, in tablature, and in rhythm slashes

RHYTHM SLASHES: are written above the stave. Strum chords in the rhythm indicated. Round noteheads indicate single notes.

THE MUSICAL STAVE: shows pitches and rhythms and is divided by lines into bars. Pitches are named after the first seven letters of the alphabet.

TABLATURE: graphically represents the guitar fingerboard. Each horizontal line represents a string, and each number represents a fret.

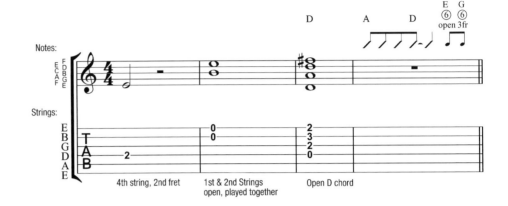

4th string, 2nd fret   1st & 2nd Strings open, played together   Open D chord

SEMI-TONE BEND: Strike the note and bend up a semi-tone (½ step).

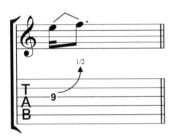

WHOLE-TONE BEND: Strike the note and bend up a whole-tone (full step).

GRACE NOTE BEND: Strike the note and bend as indicated. Play the first note as quickly as possible.

QUARTER-TONE BEND: Strike the note and bend up a ¼ step

BEND & RELEASE: Strike the note and bend up as indicated, then release back to the original note.

COMPOUND BEND & RELEASE: Strike the note and bend up and down in the rhythm indicated.

PRE-BEND: Bend the note as indicated, then strike it.

PRE-BEND & RELEASE: Bend the note as indicated. Strike it and release the note back to the original pitch.

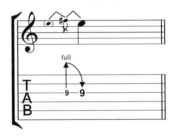

HAMMER-ON: Strike the first note with one finger, then sound the second note (on the same string) with another finger by fretting it without picking.

PULL-OFF: Place both fingers on the note to be sounded, strike the first note and without picking, pull the finger off to sound the second note.

LEGATO SLIDE (GLISS): Strike the first note and then slide the same fret-hand finger up or down to the second note. The second note is not struck.

MUFFLED STRINGS: A percussive sound is produced by laying the first hand across the string(s) without depressing, and striking them with the pick hand.

NATURAL HARMONIC: Strike the note while the fret-hand lightly touches the string directly over the fret indicated.

ARTIFICIAL HARMONIC: Fret lower note; with first finger of picking hand lightly touch string an octave above (fret position shown in parentheses) while striking string.

PERCUSSIVE NOTES: Strike body of guitar; the sound will vary depending on the area struck.

TREMOLO GLISSANDO: Strike the note rapidly then move the fretting hand down the neck.

TAP HARMONIC: The note is fretted normally and a harmonic is produced by 'slapping' or tapping the fret indicated in brackets (which will be twelve frets higher than the fretted note.)

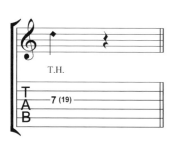

TAPPING: Hammer ('tap') the fret indicated with the pick-hand index or middle finger and pull-off to the note fretted by the fret hand.

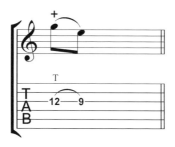

PINCH HARMONIC: The note is fretted normally and a harmonic is produced by adding the edge of the thumb or the tip of the index finger of the pick hand to the normal pick attack.

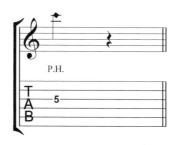

ARTIFICIAL HARMONIC: The note is fretted normally and a harmonic is produced by gently resting the pick hand's index finger directly above the indicated fret (in brackets) while plucking the appropriate string.

TRILL: Very rapidly alternate between the notes indicated by continuously hammering-on and pulling-off.

RAKE: Drag the pick across the strings with a single motion.

TREMOLO PICKING: The note is picked as rapidly and continuously as possible.

ARPEGGIATE: Play the notes of the chord indicated by quickly rolling them from bottom to top.

ADDITIONAL MUSICAL DEFINITIONS

 (accent)   Accentuate note (play it louder).

D.S. al Coda   Go back to the sign (𝄋), then play until the bar marked *To Coda* ⊕ then skip to the section marked ⊕ *Coda* .

 (accent)   Accentuate note with greater intensity.

D.C. al Fine   Go back to the beginning of the song and play until the bar marked *Fine*.

 (staccato)   Shorten time value of note.

tacet   Instrument is silent (drops out).

⊓   Downstroke

V   Upstroke

   Repeat bars between signs.

NOTE: Tablature numbers in brackets mean:
1. The note is sustained, but a new articulation (such as hammer on or slide) begins
2. A note may be fretted but not necessarily played.

    When a repeat section has different endings, play the first ending only the first time and the second ending only the second time.

1952 VINCENT BLACK LIGHTNING

Words & Music by Richard Thompson

†Symbols in parentheses represent chord names with respect to capoed guitar. Symbols above represent actual sounding chords. (TAB 0=3rd fret.)

hat's off to you,_____ it's a Vin - cent Black Light-ning, nine - teen_

_ fif - ty - two._____ And I've seen you at the cor-

- ners and____ ca - fés_____ it seems,_____ red hair and black lea-ther; my

fav -'rite col-our scheme." And he pulled_____ her on__ be -

- hind_____ and__ down to__ Box__ Hill_____

they__ did ride.

2. Oh,__ says

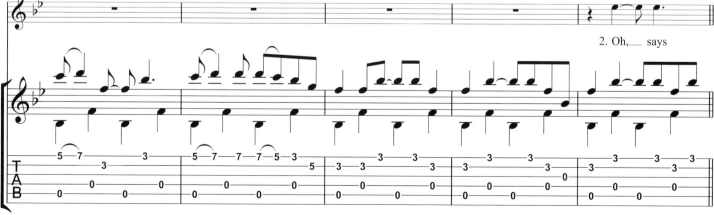

13

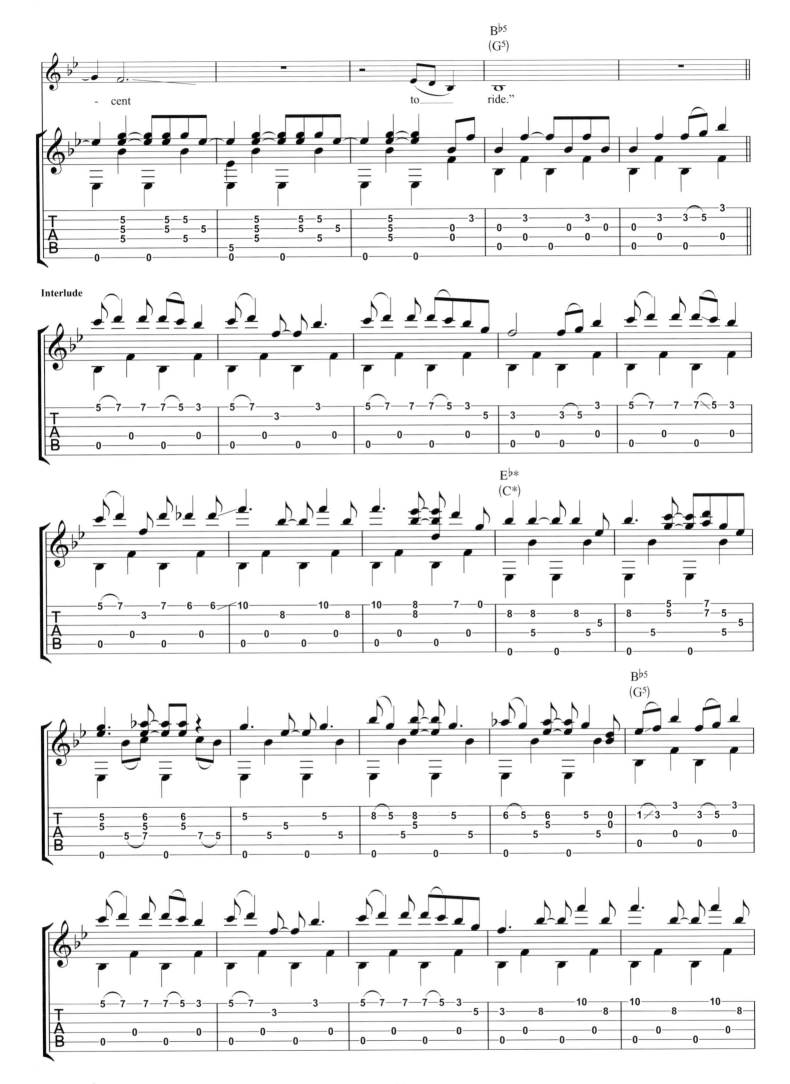

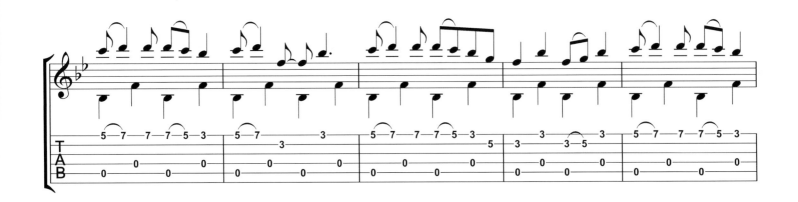

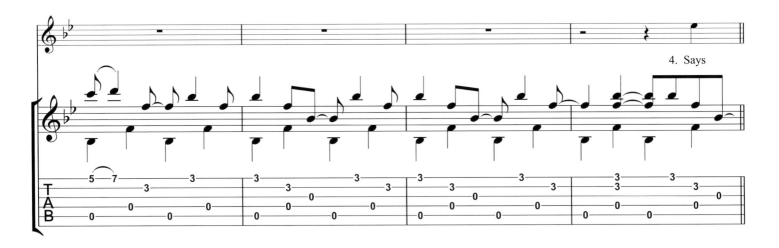

4. Says

Verse

James, "In my o - pin - ion, there's no-thing in this world

$E^\flat$
(C)

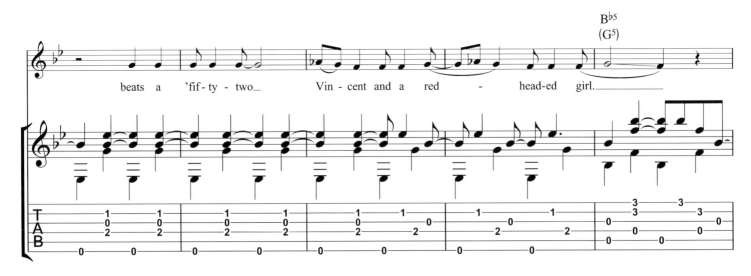

beats a 'fif-ty - two Vin - cent and a red - head-ed girl.

$B^{\flat 5}$
(G^5)

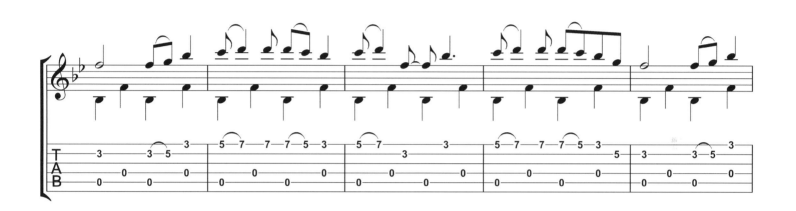

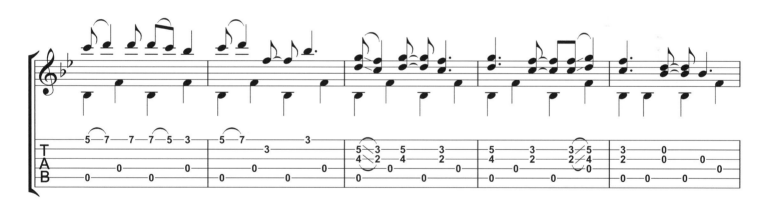

ANJI

Music by Davey Graham

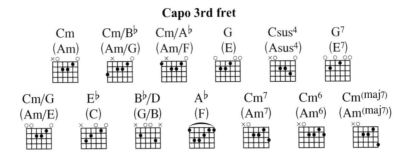

Capo 3rd fret

♩ = 152

Acoustic steel string guitar, Capo 3rd fret

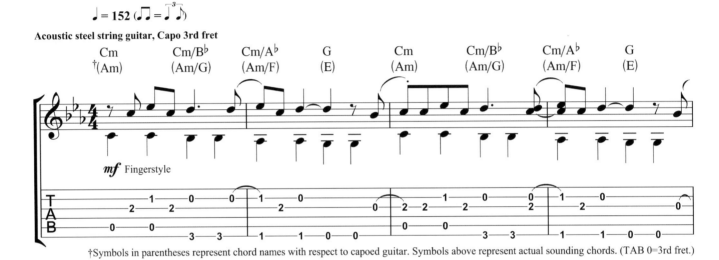

mf Fingerstyle

†Symbols in parentheses represent chord names with respect to capoed guitar. Symbols above represent actual sounding chords. (TAB 0=3rd fret.)

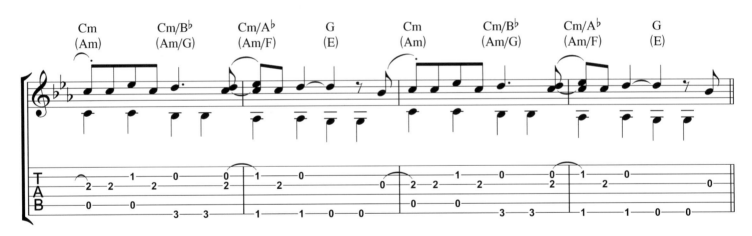

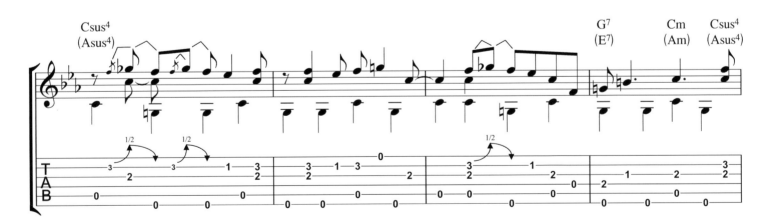

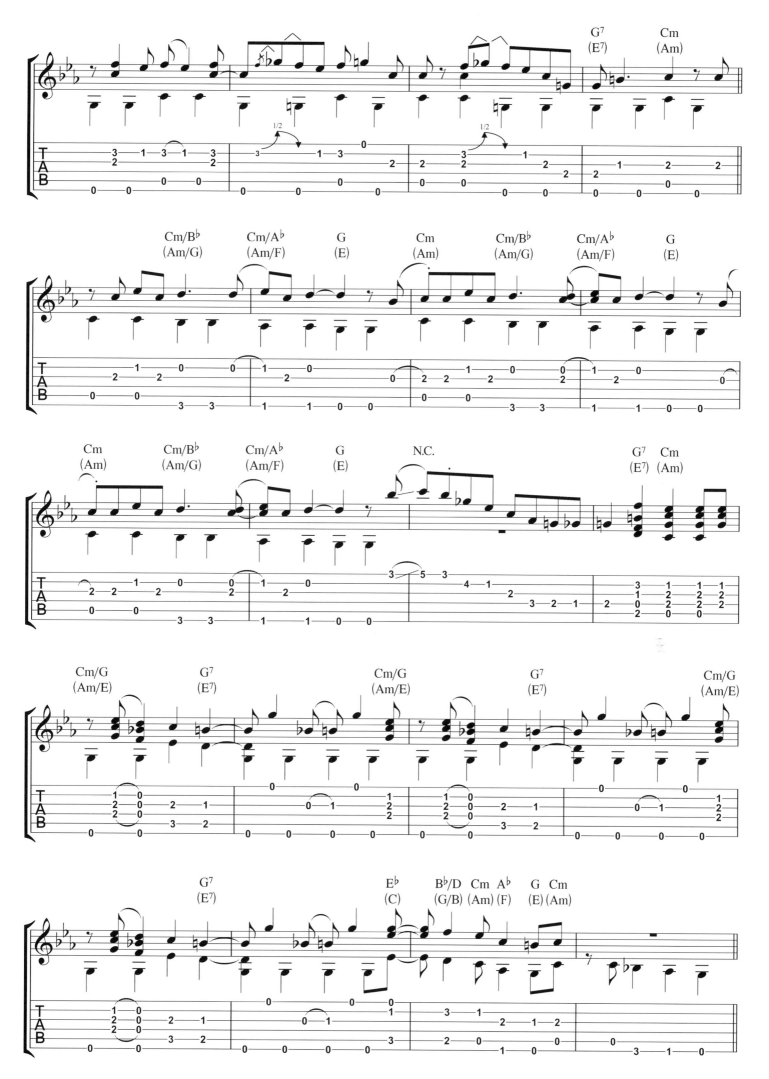

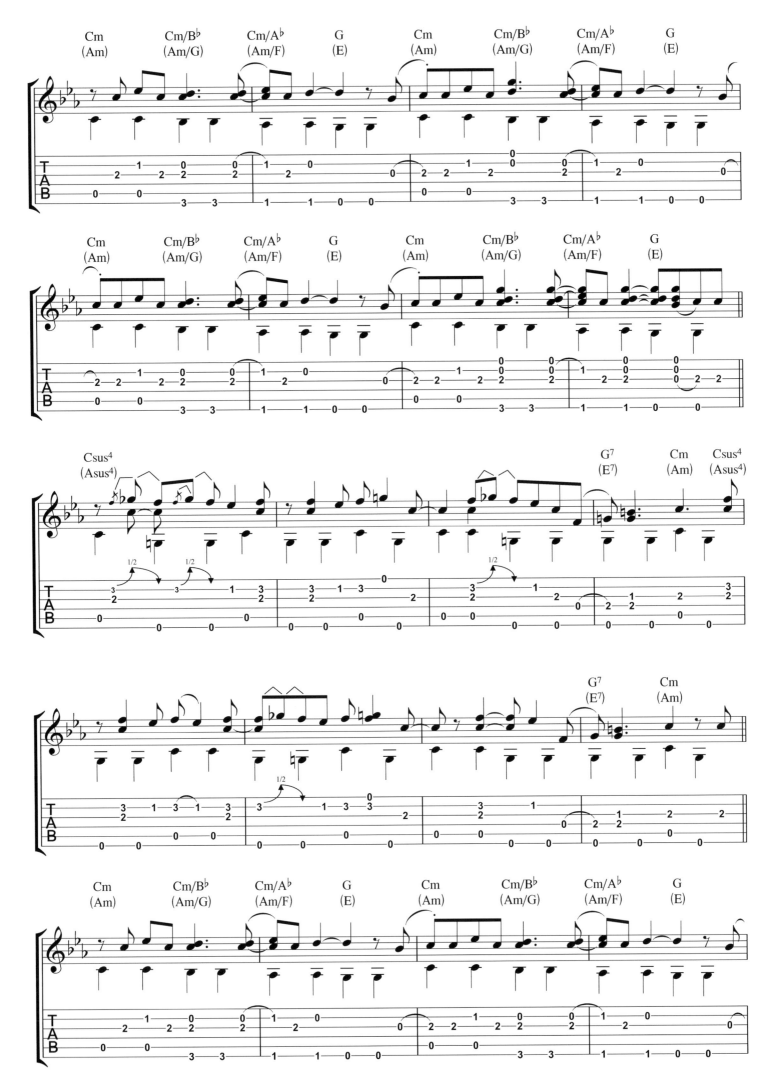

28

BLACKWATER SIDE

Traditional

Arranged by Vivian Palmer, Joseph Giltrap & Michael Simmonds

†Chord names represent implied harmony.

CANADEE-I-O

Traditional
Arranged by Nic Jones

*▼ = Percussive stroke with 3rd finger of picking hand.
†Chord names represent implied harmony.

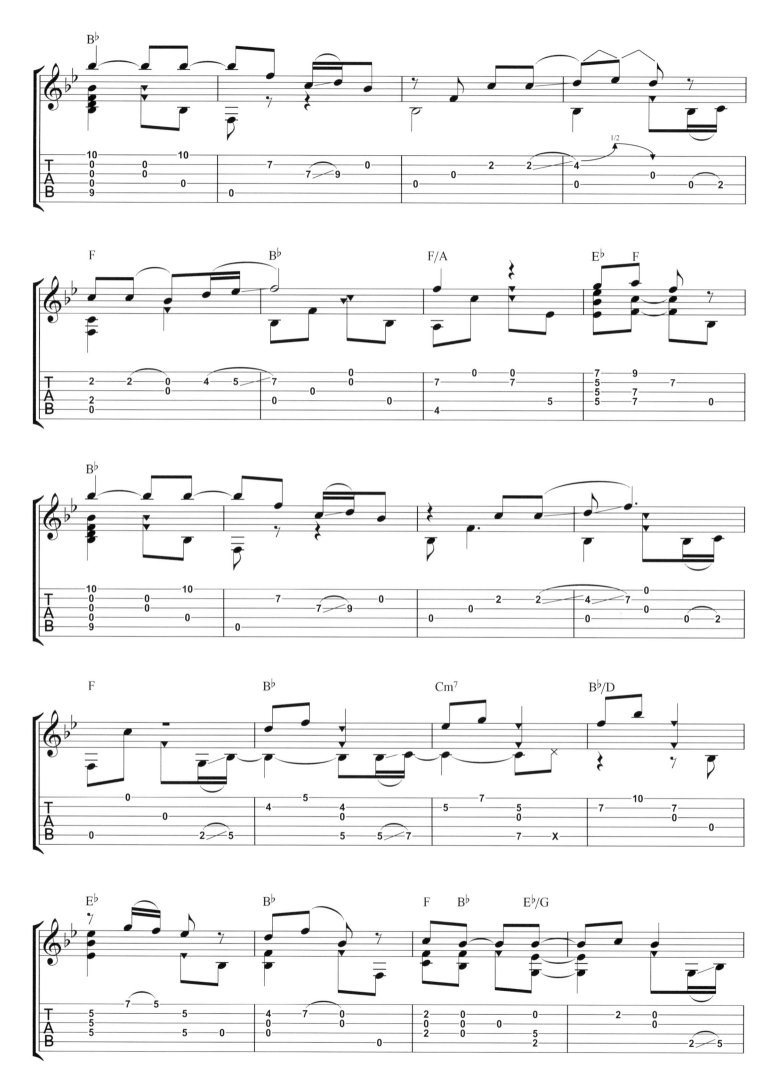

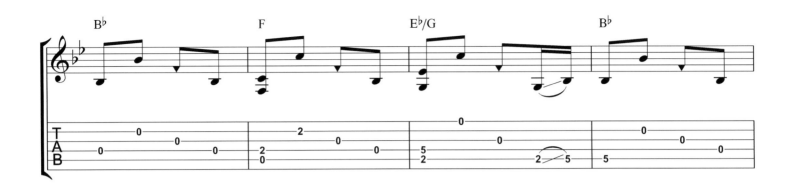

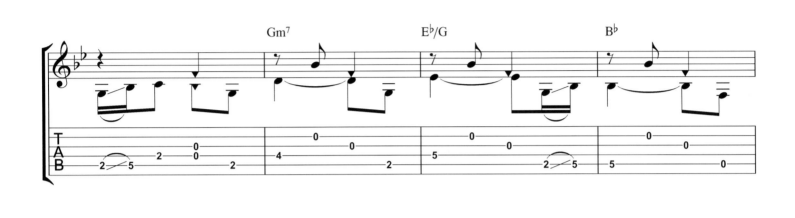

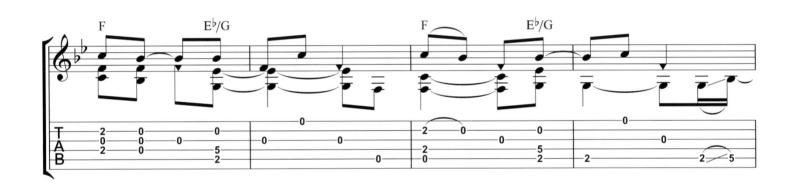

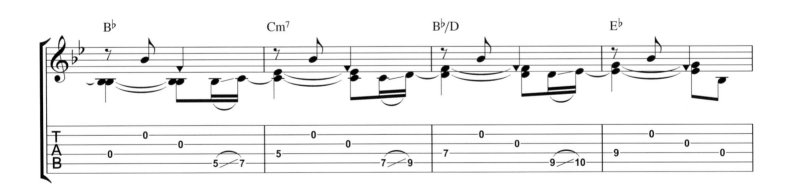

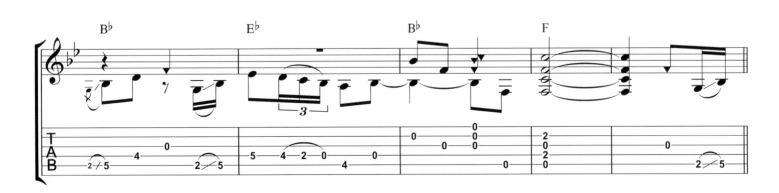

Verse

1. It's of a fair___ and hand-some girl_____ and she's all in her
(Verses 2-6 see block lyrics)

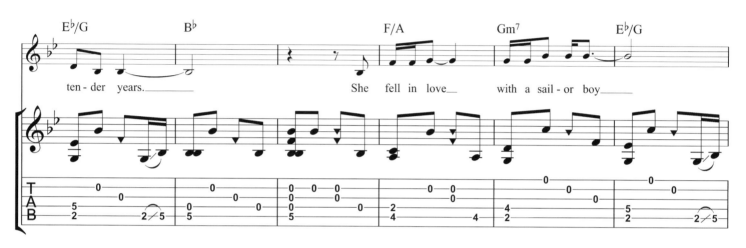

ten-der years._____ She fell in love___ with a sail-or boy_____

and it's true_____ that she loved him well,_____ for to go___ off

to sea___ with him___ like she did not___ know___ how._____

Lyrics visible in the music:

She longed to see____ that__ sea - port town____ called Ca - na - dee -
- i - o.____

To 3º, 4º, 5º, 6º endings **1.**

2.

D.S. al 3º ending

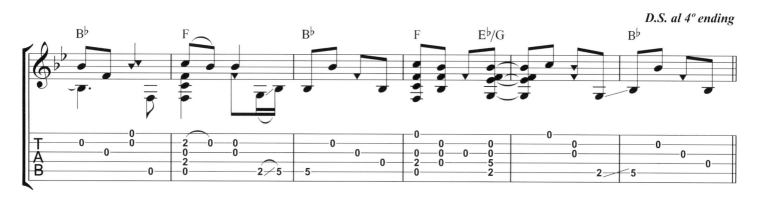

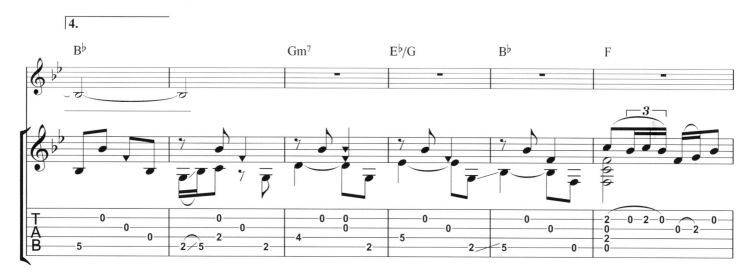

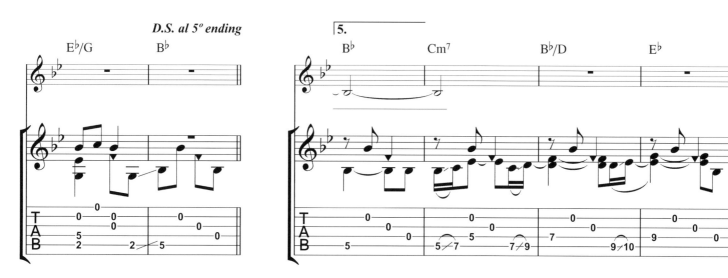

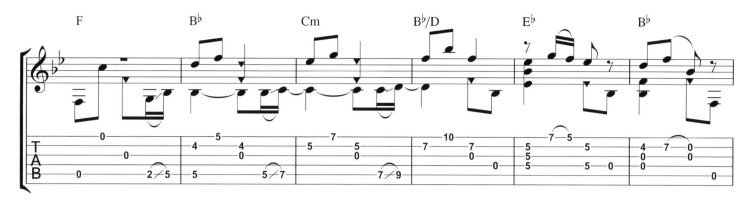

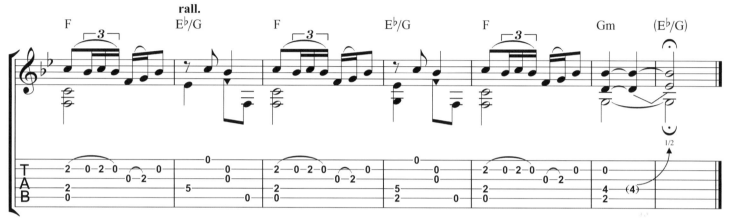

Verse 2:

So she bargained with the young sailor boy, all for a piece of gold.

Straight away then he led her all down into the hold,

Saying, "I'll dress you up in sailor's clothes, your jacket shall be blue.

And you'll see that seaport town called Canadee-i-o."

Verse 3:

Now, when the other sailors heard the news, well, they fell into a rage.

And with all the whole ship's company they were willing to engage.

Saying, "We'll tie her hands and feet, me boys, overboard we'll throw her.

And she'll never see that seaport town called Canadee-i-o."

Verse 4:

Now, when the captain he's heard the news, well, he too fell in a rage.

And with all of his whole ship's company he was willing to engage.

Saying, "She'll stay all in sailor's clothes, her collar shall be blue,

She'll see that seaport town called Canadee-i-o."

Verse 5:

Now, when they came down to Canada scarcely above half a year,

She's married this bold captain who called her his dear.

She's dressed in silks and satins now and she cuts a gallant show,

She's the finest of the ladies down in Canadee-i-o.

Verse 6:

Come, all you fair and tender girls, wheresoever you may be,

I'd have you to follow your own true love when he goes out on the sea.

For if the sailors prove false to you, well, the captain, he might prove true.

You see the honour that I have gained by the wearing of the blue.

THE HERMIT

Music by John Renbourn

41

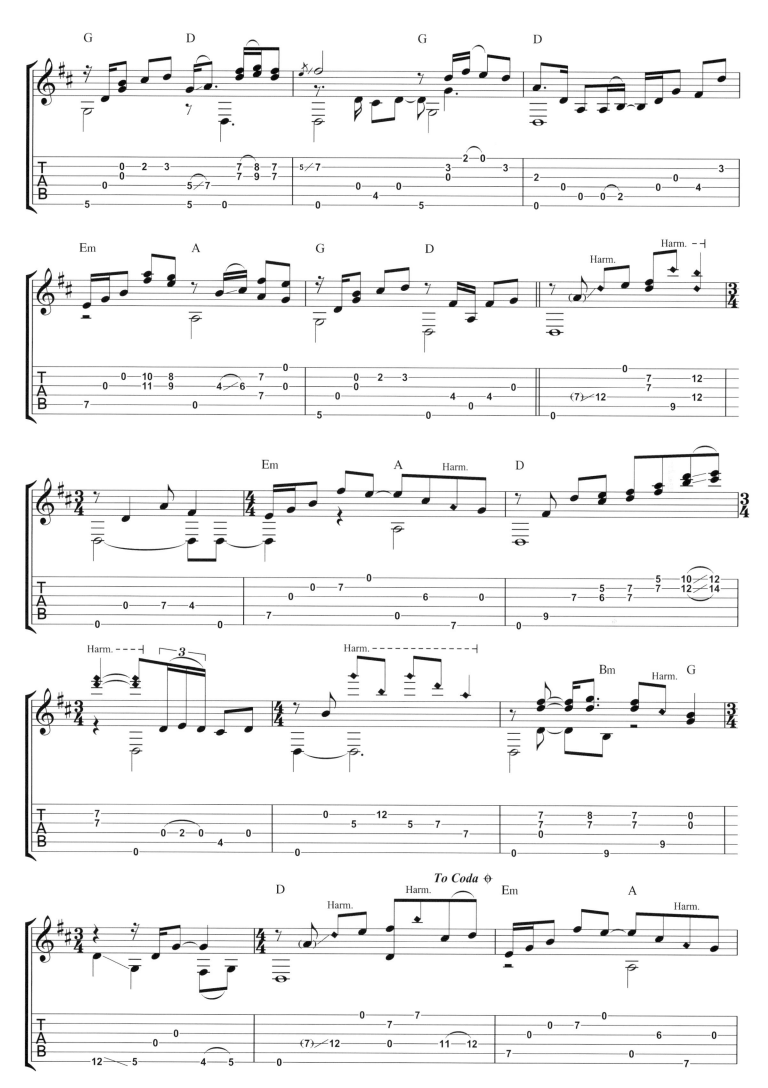

43

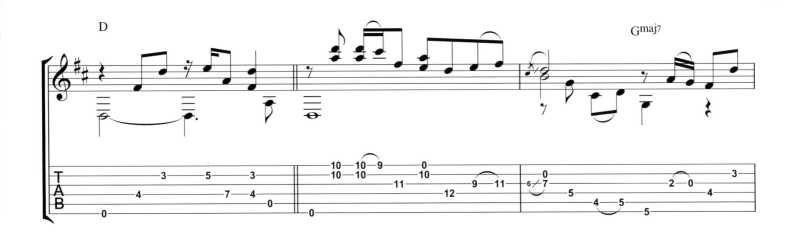

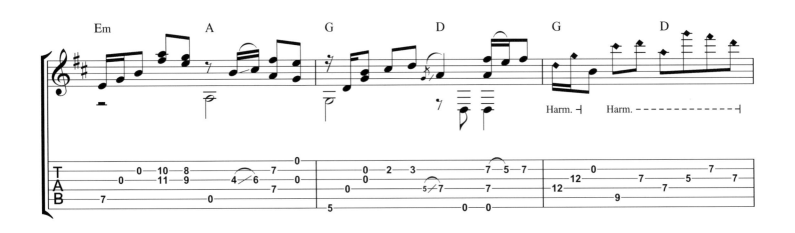

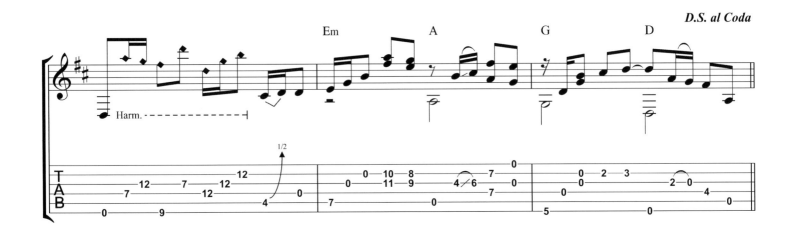

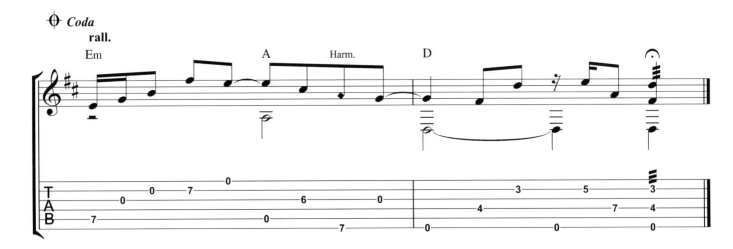

MAY YOU NEVER

Words & Music by John Martyn

* Gently slap palm of hand against string to give a damped percussive effect.
†Symbols in parentheses represent chord names with respect to capoed guitar.
Symbols above represent actual sounding chords. (TAB 0=2nd fret.)

*percussive hits with left hand on fretboard

47

Love is a les-son to learn in our time — and please, won't you please, won't you

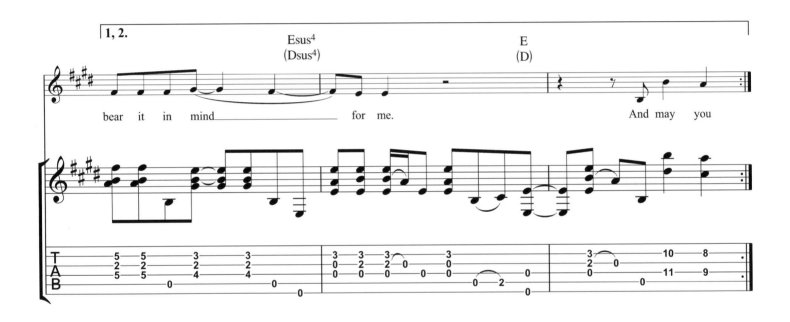

bear it in mind _____ for me. And may you

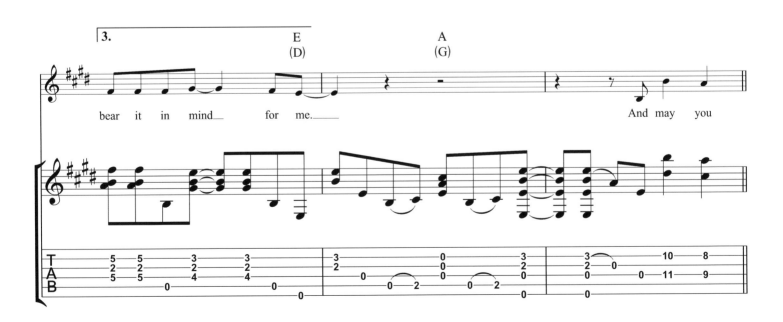

bear it in mind ____ for me. ____ And may you

48

ne - ver lose your tem - per if you get___ in a bar - room fight,___

___ and may___ you ne - ver lose your wo - man ov - er - night.___

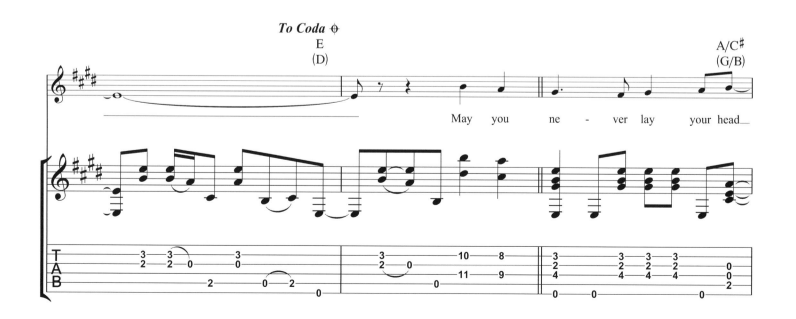

May you ne - ver lay your head___

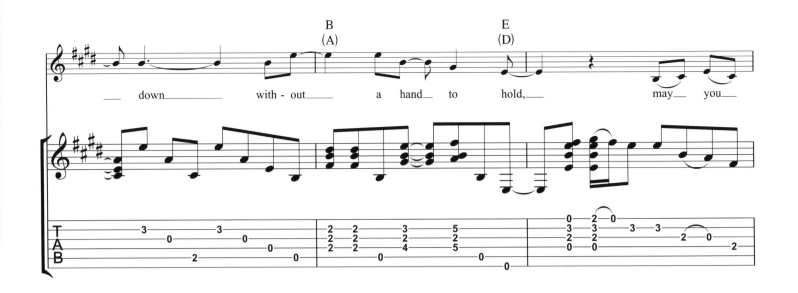

down_____ with - out_____ a hand__ to hold,_____ may__ you_____

D.S. al Coda

ne - ver make your bed___ out__ in___ the cold._____ May you___

✛ *Coda*

___ May__ you ne - ver lose your wo - man ov - er - night,___

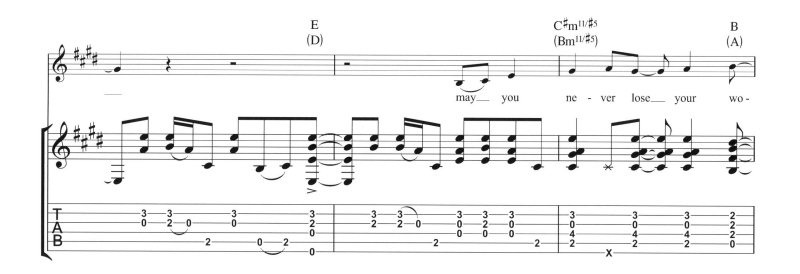

may__ you ne - ver lose__ your wo -

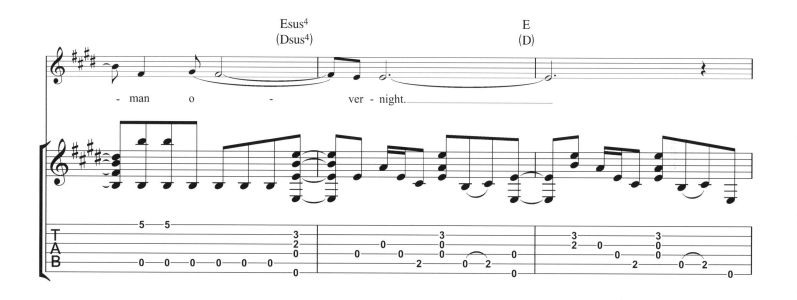

- man o - ver - night._____

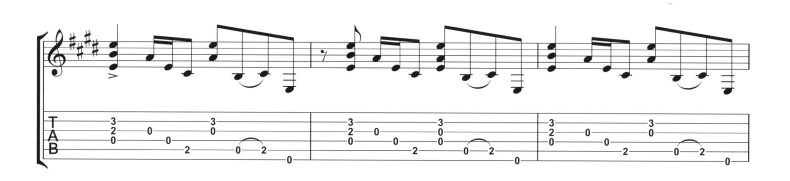

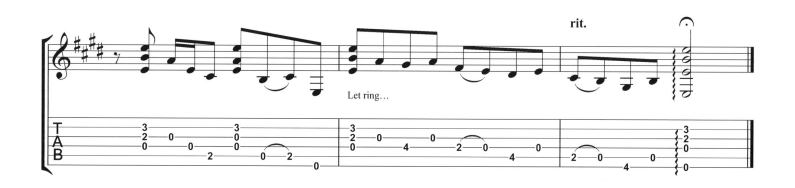

Let ring…

MY BABY SO SWEET

Words & Music by Jimmy Reed

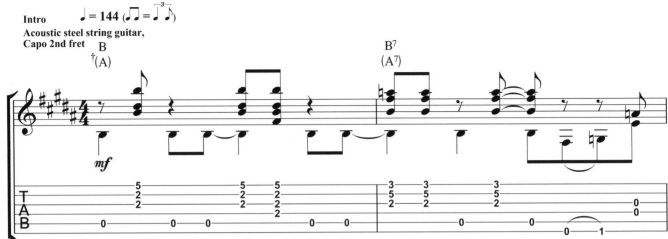

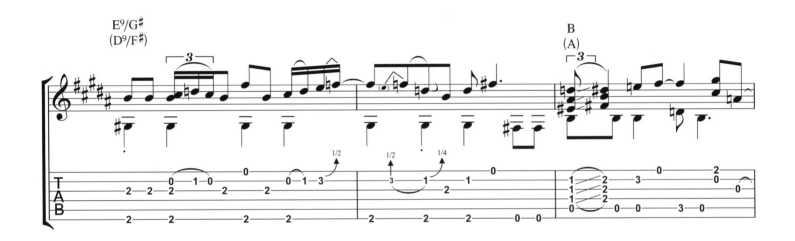

†Symbols in parentheses represent chord names with respect to capoed guitar.
Symbols above represent actual sounding chords. (TAB 0=2nd fret.)

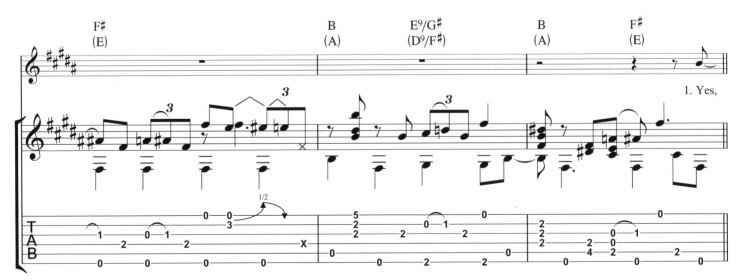

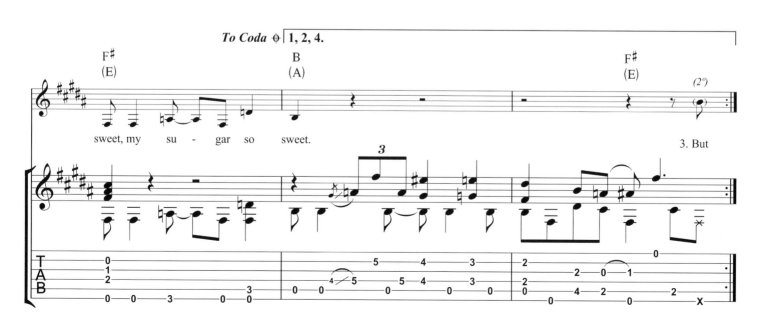

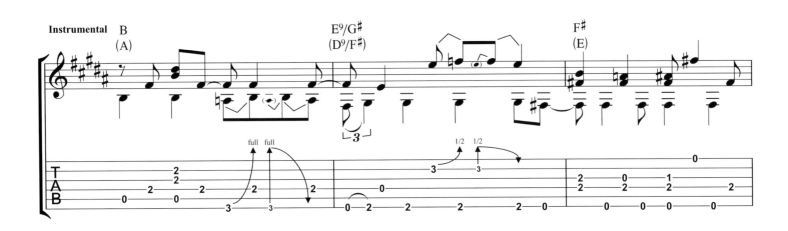

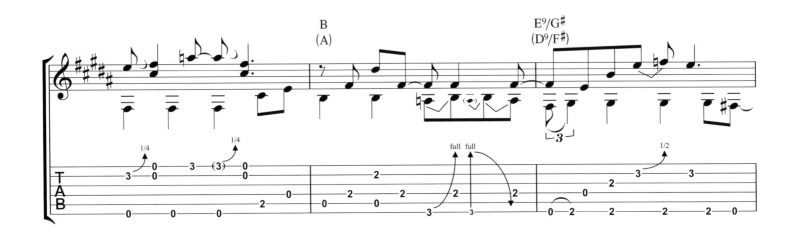

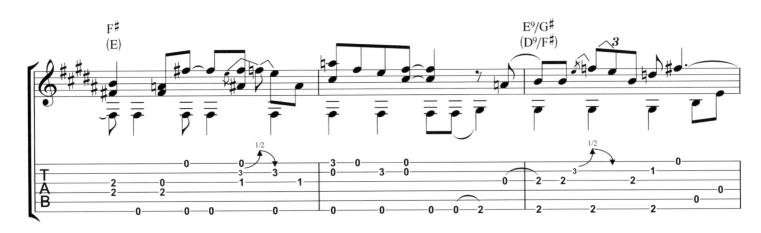

D.S. al Coda

Verse 4:
See my baby, don't act so smart,
I'll cut out your liver, eat your heart.
So sweet, so sweet, my sugar so sweet.

Verse 5:
Yes, mama, yes, girl,
Hear me calling you.
So sweet, so sweet, my sugar so sweet.

ON AGAIN! ON AGAIN!

Words & Music by Jake Thackray

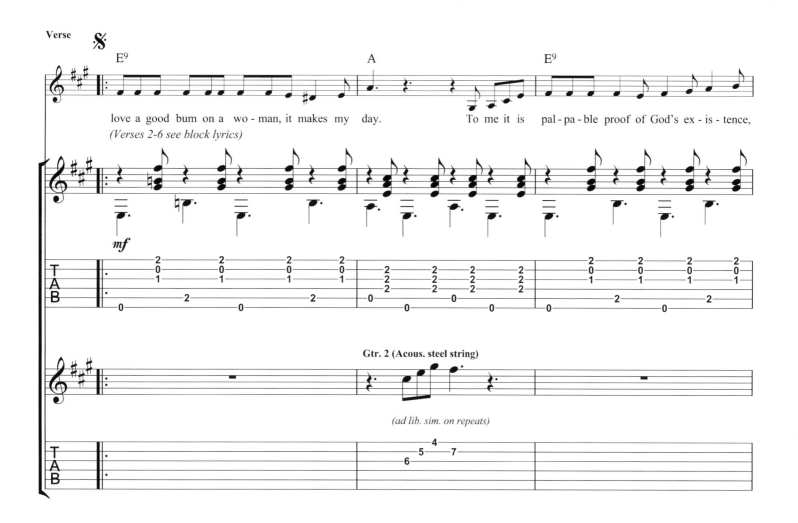

tongue, the tongue, the tongue on a wo-man that spoils the job for me. Please un-der-

-stand I re-spect and ad-mire the frail-er sex, and I ho-nour them ev-e-ry bit as much as the

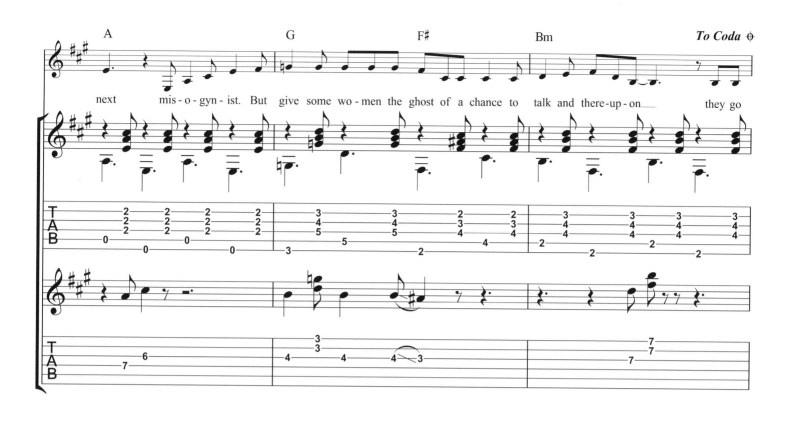

next mis-o-gyn-ist. But give some wo-men the ghost of a chance to talk and there-up-on___ they go

on a-gain, on a-gain, on a-gain, on a-gain, on a-gain, on a-gain, on.

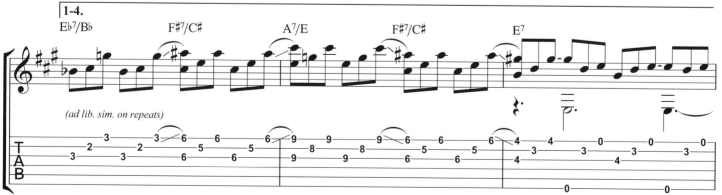

(ad lib. sim. on repeats)

on a - gain, on a - gain, on a - gain, on a - gain. And a -

- gain, and a - gain, and a - gain, and a - gain. They will go

Verse 2:
I fell in love with a woman with wonderful thighs and hips
And a sensational belly, I just never noticed her lips were always moving.
Only when we got to the altar and she had to say "I do."
And she folded her arms and gathered herself and took in a breath and I knew
She could have gone on again, on again, on again till the entire
Congregation passed out and the vicar passed on and the
    choirboys passed through puberty.
At the reception I gloomily noted her family's jubilant mood,
Their maniacal laughter and their ghastly gratitude.

Verse 3:
She talks to me when I go for a shave or a sleep or a swim.
She talks to me on a Sunday when I go singing hymns and drinking heavily.
When I go mending my chimney pot she's down there in the street,
And at ninety-five on my motorbike she's on the pillion seat
Wittering on again, on again, on and again and again.
When I'm eating or drinking or reading or thinking or when
    I'm saying my rosary.
She will never stop talking to me; she is one of those women who
Will never use three or four words when a couple of thousand will easily do!

Verse 4:
She also talks without stopping to me in our bed of a night;
Throughout the sweetest of our intimate delights she never gives over.
Not even stopping while we go hammer and tongs towards the peak –
Except maybe for a sigh and a groan and one perfunctory shriek.
Then she goes on again, on again, on again on and I must
Assume that she has never noticed that she's just been interrupted.
Totally unruffled she is, and as far as I can see
I might just as well have been posting a letter or stirring up the tea!

Verse 5:
She will not take a hint, not once she's made a start.
I can yawn or belch or bleed or faint or fart – she'll not drop a syllable.
I could stand in front of her grimly sharpening up an axe,
I could sprinkle her with paraffin, and ask her for a match –
She'd just go on again, on again, on again even more.
The hind leg off a donkey is peanuts for her, she can bore
    the balls off a buffalo.
"Mother of God," I cried one day, "Oh, let your kingdom come,
And in the meantime, Mother, could you strike this bugger dumb?"

Verse 6:
Well, believe it or not, she appeared to me then and there:
The Blessed Virgin herself, in answer to my prayer, despite the vulgarity,
Shimmering softly, dressed in blue and holding up a hand.
I cocked a pious ear as the Mother of God began.
Well she went on again, on again, on again, on, and I
Will have to state how very much I sympathise with the rest of the family.
Give some women the ghost of a chance to talk and thereupon
They go on again, on again, on again, on again,
And again, and again, and again, and again
They will go on again, on again, on again, on again, on again, on again, on.

STROLLING DOWN THE HIGHWAY

Words & Music by Bert Jansch

Capo 5th fret

Intro

♩ = 126

Acoustic steel string guitar, capo 5th fret.

mf Played with thumb-pick and fingers.

†Symbols in parentheses represent chord names with respect to capoed guitar. Symbols above represent actual sounding chords. (TAB 0=5th fret.)

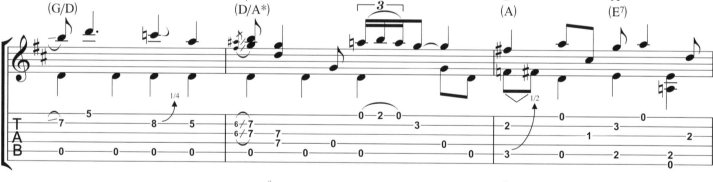

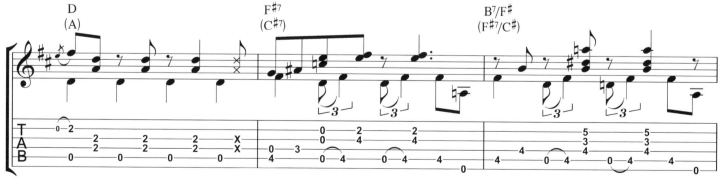

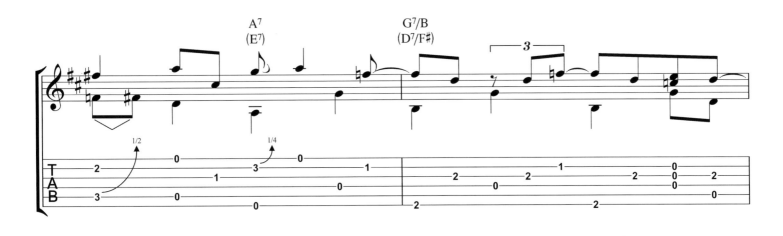

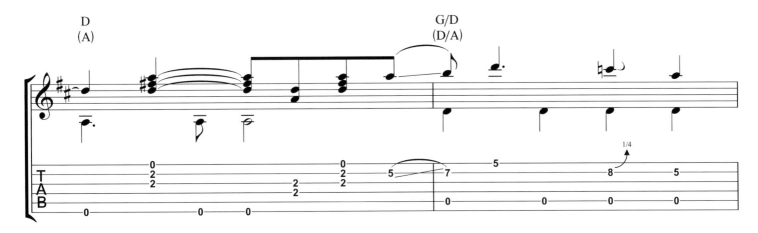

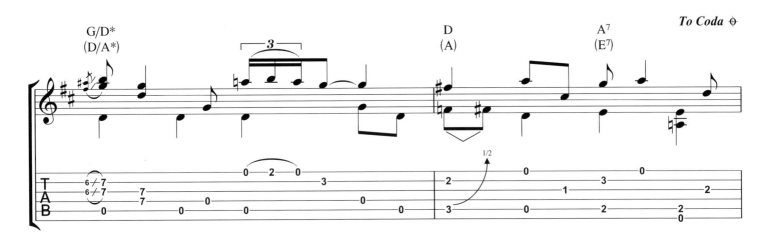

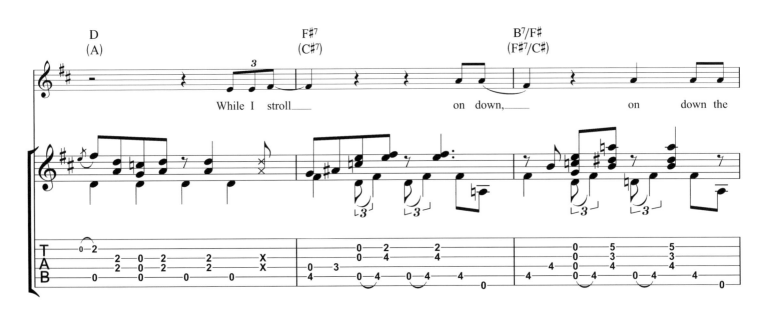

While I stroll___ on down,___ on down the

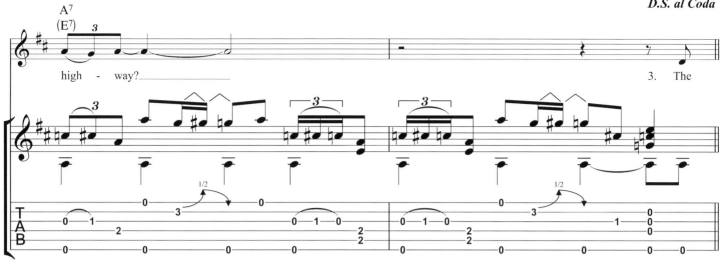

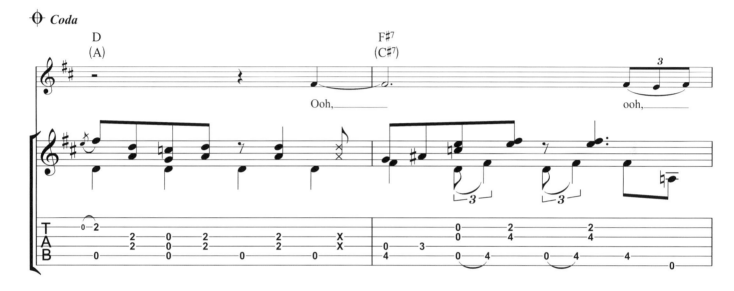

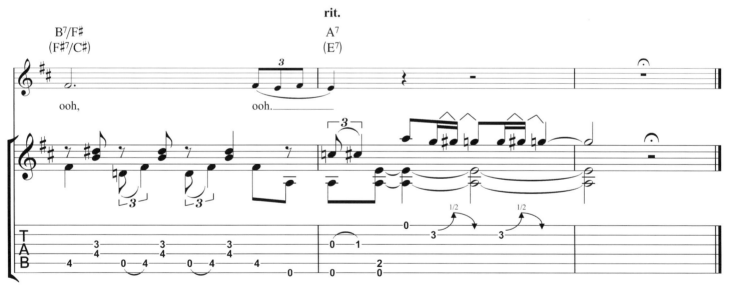

Verse 3:
The cars won't stop for no one,
They don't think, your just rollin' bum.
They think you're an O.A.S. spy,
Gonna shoot them as a they go by.
No, the cars they won't stop, won't stop for no one.

THE WHALE CATCHERS

Traditional
Arranged by Martin Carthy

Tuning*
6 = C 3 = D
5 = G 2 = G
4 = C 1 = A

*To match original recording tune slightly flat

Intro $\quad \downarrow = 160$

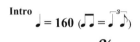

Acoustic steel string guitar

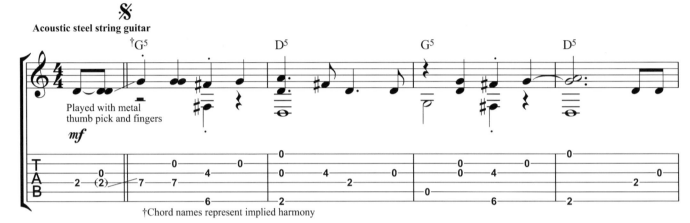

Played with metal thumb pick and fingers

mf

†Chord names represent implied harmony

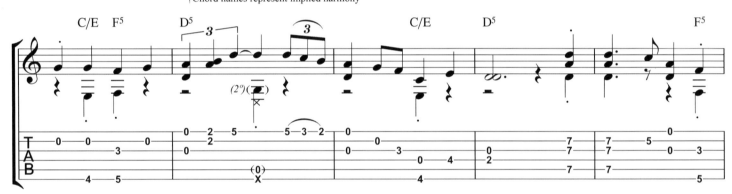

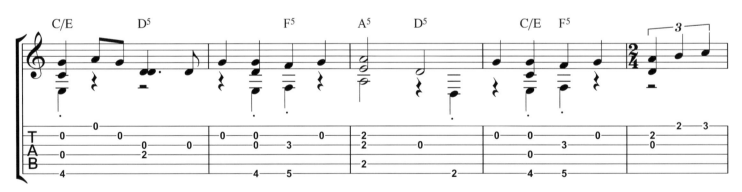

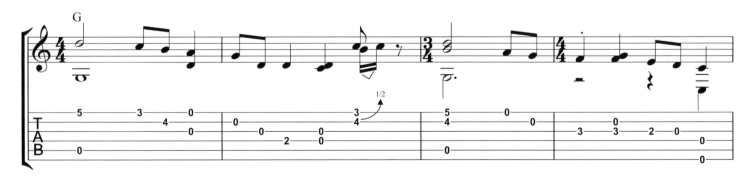

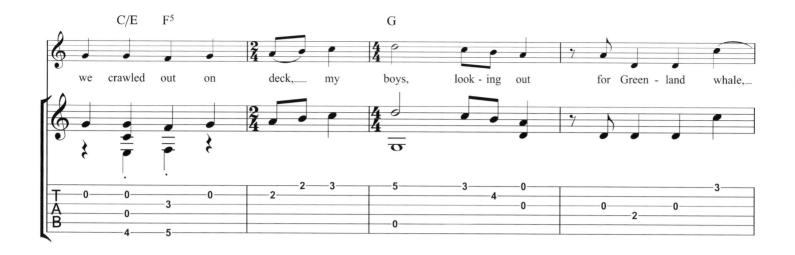

we crawled out on deck,___ my boys, look-ing out for Green-land whale,___

look-ing out for Green-land whale.

D.S. al Coda

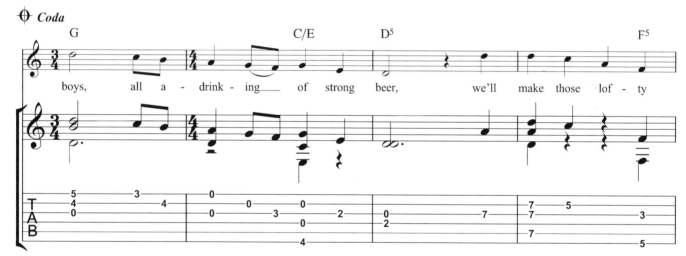

Coda

boys, all a - drink-ing___ of strong beer, we'll make those lof-ty

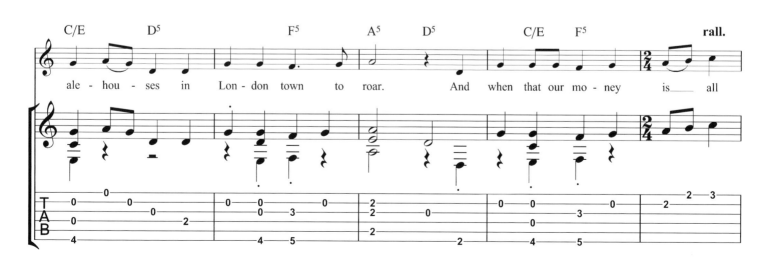

ale - hou - ses in Lon-don town to roar. And when that our mo-ney is___ all

gone   to   Green - land   go   for   more,   to   Green - land   go   for   more.